A RED CHERRY ON
A WHITE-TILED FLOOR

MARAM AL-MASSRI

A Red Cherry on a White-tiled Floor

SELECTED POEMS

translated by
KHALED MATTAWA

BLOODAXE BOOKS

ISBN: 1 85224 640 5

First published 2004 by
Bloodaxe Books Ltd,
Highgreen,
Tarset,
Northumberland NE48 1RP.

www.bloodaxebooks.com
For further information about Bloodaxe titles
please visit our website or write to
the above address for a catalogue.

Bloodaxe Books Ltd acknowledges
the financial assistance of
Arts Council England, North East.

Cover printing by J. Thomson Colour Printers Ltd, Glasgow.

Printed in Great Britain by
Cromwell Press Ltd, Trowbridge, Wiltshire.

ACKNOWLEDGEMENTS

This book presents a selection of poems from two book-length sequences. The first, *Karzatun Hamraa ala Balatin Abyad* (A Red Cherry on a White-tiled Floor), was published by Éditions de L'or du temps, Tunis, in 1997; the second, *Andhur Elaik* (I Look to You), was published by La Société d'Éditions et de Publication, Beirut, in 2000. Some of the translations have appeared in *Banipal, Lyric Poetry Review* (USA) and *Rattapallax* (USA).

Special thanks are due to Arts Council England for providing a translation grant for this book.

CONTENTS

A Red Cherry on
a White-tiled Floor

Karzatun Hamraa
ala Balatin Abyad

(1997)

1

أنا سارقة السَّكَاكِر ،
أمام دكانك
دَبَّقْتْ أصابعي ،
ولم أنجح
بوضع واحدة في
فمي .

I am the thief
of sweetmeats
displayed in your shop.
My fingers became sticky
but I failed
to drop one
into my mouth.

2

يا للغباء
قلبي في كل مرة يسمع نقراً
يَفْتَح .

How foolish:
Whenever my heart
hears a knocking
it opens its doors.

3

تُشْعِلني الرغبة
وتتألق عيناي .
أحشر الأخلاق في أقرب دُرج ،
أتقمص الشيطان ،
وأَعْصُب عيون ملائكتي
من أجل
قُبلة .

Desire inflames me
and my eyes glimmer.
I stuff morals
in the nearest drawer,
I turn into The Devil
and blindfold my angels
just
for a kiss.

5

أنتظر ،
وماذا أنتظر ؟
رجلاً يأتي محملاً بالزهور ،
وبكلمات جميلة .
رجلاً
ينظر إلي ويراني .
يحدثني ويسمعني .
رجلاً يبكي
لأجلي ،
فأشفق عليه
وأحبه .

I wait,
but what do I wait for?
A man who brings me flowers
and sweet words,
a man
who looks at me and sees me.
He talks to me and listens to me.
A man who weeps
for me
and I pity him
and I love him.

6

رأيت أثار
الأقدام
نقاطاً سوداء
ذاهبة آتيه .
الثلج الأبيض
الذي قيل عنه
نقي ،
فضح
العصافير والقطط
وأشباح أفكاري ،
قبل أن تأتي الشمس الكسولة ،
لتمحو
كل ذلك .

I saw
foot traces,
black spots
coming and going.
The white snow,
they said
was pure,
betrayed
the sparrows and cats
and the ghosts of my thoughts
before the lazy sun rose
and erased them
all.

7

طرقات على الباب .	Knocks on the door.
من ؟	Who?
أوري غُبار وحدتي	I sweep the dust of my loneliness
تحت سجّادتي ،	under the rug.
أرتِّب ابتسامتي ،	I arrange a smile
وأفتح .	and open.

8

غريب ينظر إليّ ،	A stranger looks at me,
غريب يحدثني ،	a stranger speaks to me.
لغريب أبتسم ،	To a stranger I smile,
لغريب أتحدث ،	to a stranger I speak.
غريب يسمعني ،	A stranger listens to me
أمام	and at
أحزانه البيضاء النظيفة	his clean white sorrows
أبكي ؛	I weep
للوحدة التي تجمع	to the loneliness that gathers
الغرباء .	strangers.

9

يدخلون حياتنا
كالجداول الصغيرة ،
فاذا بنا
نغرق بهم ،
ولا نعود نعرف
من أعطانا
ماءً وملحاً ،
ومن ترك
فينا تلك
المرارة .

They enter our lives
like small streams
and suddenly
we drown in them
and become unaware
of who gave us
water and salt
and left in us
that
bitterness.

11

وحدها
لم أدْعُها ،
تجيء لزيارتي .
تحوم حولي
أطرُدُها ،
فاذا بها
كذُبابة سوداء
كذبابة سوداء بشعة
تطير هنا ، تطن هناك
وتحط في قعر قلبي .
الكآبة
بقرة بلهاء ،
تجترّ
الأخضر واليابس
من غبطتي .

Alone –
I never let her
visit me.
She hovers around me
and I kick her out.
Then she becomes
like a black fly,
an ugly black fly,
zips here, buzzes there,
and lands in the bottom of my heart.
Melancholy
a crazed cow
devours
the green and dry
shoots of my ecstasy.

12

دقيقة على جانبي
الأيسر .
دقيقة على جانبي
الأيمن .
قليلا على ظهري ،
برهةً على بطني .
أدور في الفراغ
بردٌ في أحلامي
بردٌ في سريري .
لصوص النوم غزوا ليلتي ؛
واحدٌ منهم
أشفق عليّ
وترك لي الصباح
على الطاولة .

A minute on my left
side,
a minute on my right
side,
a little on my back,
a while on my stomach,
I spin in emptiness.
Cold in my bed.
Cold in my dreams.
The thieves of sleep
have raided my night,
One of them
pitied me
and left me the morning
shining on the table.

13

من أين يأتي هذا الغبار ؟
من أين يأتي ؟
تمر بكفك عليه لتمحوه
لكنه دائماً يعود
كالوجوه
كالأصوات .
تظنه يتوسد السطوح
وإذا به يملأ الأعماق .

من أين تأتي هذه الذكريات
من أين تأتي ...

Where does this dust come from?
Where from?
You pass your palm over it to wipe it,
but it always returns
like the faces,
like the voices.
You think it only covers surfaces,
but it turns to fill the depths.

Where do these memories come from?
Where do they come from?

14

النساءُ مثلي
لا يَعْرِفْنَ الكلامَ ؛
الكلمةُ تبقى في الحلق
كالشوكة ،
يُفضّلْنَ بلعَها .
النساءُ مثلي
لا يعرفن سوى البُكاء ،
البكاء المستعصي
فجأة
ينهمر
كشريان مقطوع .
النساء مثلي
تَتَلَقّيْنَ الصفعات ،
ولا يجرُؤْن على ردّها .
يرتجفن من الغضب
يكبحْنَه .
كأسد في قفص
النساءُ مثلي
يحلمن ...
... بالحرية ...

Women like me
do not know how to speak.
A word remains in their throats
like a thorn
they choose to swallow.
Women like me
know nothing except weeping,
impossible weeping
suddenly
pouring
like a severed artery.
Women like me
receive blows
and do not dare return them.
They shake with anger,
they subdue it.
Like lions in cages,
women like me
dream...
of freedom...

16

إنها تفتح لي
أبوابها العريضة .
إنها تناديني
وتدفعني لأن أطلق
نفسي في
فضائها ،
وكعُصْفور
أمام باب قفصه المفتوح
لا أجرؤ .

It opens
its wide doors to me.
It calls me
and nudges me forward
to release myself
into its space,
and like a sparrow
at the gate of its open cage
I do not dare.

17

حيث الأحصنه
لا تستطيع الركض .
حيث لا يوجد
ثغرة
تسمح
لشعاع من الضوء أن يدخل .
حيث لا عشب
ينبتُ ؛
أتشبث
بأقدام الكلمة

Where horses
cannot gallop,
where there is no
crack
to allow
a beam of light to pass,
where no grass
grows,
I cling
to the feet of the word.

19

أربطها	I tie it
بين الفك والحنك	between jaw and chin
بقماشة بيضاء	with white cloth.
أشدها وراء رقبتي	I drag it from the back of my neck
كالموتى	like the dead,
كالسجناء	like prisoners,
لئلا	so it would not
تَدْوي .	resound.

20

قتلت أبي	I killed my father
تلك الليلة	that night
أو ذاك النهار	or the other day –
لم أعد أدري ،	I don't remember.
هاربة بحقيبة واحدة	I escape with a suitcase
ملأتُها بأحلامٍ دونَ ذاكرة ،	filled with dreams and amnesia
وبصورة لي	and a picture of me
معه	with him
وأنا صغيرة	when I was a child
يحملني	and when he carried me
على زنده .	on his forearm.

دفنت أبي	I buried my father
في صَدَفَةٍ جميلة	in a beautiful shell,
في محيطٍ عميق ،	in a deep ocean,
لكنه وجدني	but he found me
مختبئةً تحت السرير	hiding under the bed
أرتجف من الخوف	shaking with fear
والوحدة .	and loneliness.

21

في كل مرة
أفتح حقيبتي
يخرج غبار .

Each time
I open my bag
dust blows out of it.

22

طلبتْ منه
حُلماً ،
فوهبها حقيقة .
من يومها
وجدت نفسها
ثكلى .

She asked him
for a dream
and he offered her a reality.
Since then
she found herself
a bereaved mother.

23

سأنتظر
أن ينام الأطفال ،
لأتْرُك
جُثَّة خيبتي
تطفو
على السطح .

I will wait
until the children sleep
then let
the corpse of my failure
float
to the roof.

24

غُط في نومكَ ،
ولا تُعِر انتباهاً
لسُهادي ،
اَتركني أحلُم قليلاً
بطرقات مشجرة
وسهول شاسعة ،
أنطلق فيها
بأحصنتي الشَبِقَة .
أنا المرأة التي عَليها أن تكونَ
عاقلةً ،
ورزينة ،
في الصباح .

Deepen you sleep
and pay no mind
to my insomnia.
Let me dream a little
of tree-lined roads
and wide meadows
that I run through
on my wild horses.
I am the woman who has to be
reasonable
and poised
in the morning.

26

اشترى
يوماً
دمية ،
تبتسم إذا أمرها بالإبتسام ،
تغني وترقص
إذا ضغط زرها ،
وتنام إذا مددها .
يا لغضبه ؛
الدمية أحياناً
تبكي ،
وأحياناً تظل فاتحة عينيها
وهي مُمَدَّدة .

One day
he bought
a doll.
She smiled
when he ordered her to smile,
she sang and danced
when he pressed her button,
and slept
when he laid her down.
But O his rage!
The doll
laid out in his bed
sometimes weeps
and stares with wide open eyes.

27

نظرت إليه
عبرَ خيطٍ من الضوء
آت
من شباك رحمتي .
الجسدُ المتعب
الذي يتمدد قربي
جائعاً مثلي .
أشرت ليَدي أن
تقترب ،
فلم تطاوعني .
أمرتها
فعاندتني .
أجبرتها .
اقتربت مرتجفة من الألم
للمْس
جَسد آخر .

I looked at him
through a thread of light
beaming from
the window of my mercy –
the tired body
spread beside me
hungry like mine.
I signalled to my hand
to come closer
and it refused,
I commanded it
and it disobeyed.
I forced it,
then bent closer
shivering with the pain
of touching
another body.

28

جسد المرأة
ينتفض على حافة سرير .

عطشٌ ..
ونهرٌ ما يفيض .

عطشٌ ..
ونبع ما يترقرق .

جسد المرأة يشيخ .
أصابع الضجر
لا تنعشه ،
والرعشة
لا تمنحه الضوء .

A woman's body
trembles on the edge of the bed.

Thirst
    and somewhere a river floods.

Thirst
    and a stream trickles.

A woman's body ages.
The fingers of boredom
do not refresh it
and the tremors
give it no light.

29

أعطني
حباً
كفاف يومي ،
ولا تثقل على قلبي الحزين
بمثقال ذرة .
خذني
ولا تضربني بوردة .
غضّ الطرف
عن أخطائي ،
وابعث برسل
قبل أن تطأ أرضي .

Give me
love
for daily rations
and don't burden my sad heart
even with a single atom.
Take me
and don't strike me with a rose.
Lower your gaze
before my errors
and send prophets
before you tread my earth.

30

ساعدني يا زوجي الطيب
أن أغلق
هذه الكوّة
التي انفتحت
في أعلى حائط
صدري .

إمنعني يا زوجي الحكيم
أن أعتلي
كَعْبَ أُنوثتي ،
فعند مفرق الطريق
شاب
ينتظرني .

Help me
my kind husband,
to close this port-hole
that has opened
on the highest wall
of my chest.

Stop me, my wise husband,
from climbing
the high-heels of my femininity,
for there at the crossroads
a young man
awaits me.

31

إمرأة تعود
برائحة رجل غريب
إلى دارها .
تغتسل ،
تتعطّر .
تبقى فوّاحةً
رائحة الندم .

A wife returns
with the scent of a man
to her home.
She washes,
she puts on perfume,
but it remains pungent,
the smell of regret.

33

لا شيء أكثر
كآبة
من رؤية
رجل وإمرأة
والملل ثالثهما .
رجل وإمرأة
قد خمدت أحلامهما ،
ولم تعد هناك أشياء بلا أهميه
يقولانها .

Nothing more
depressing
than seeing
a man and a woman,
boredom their third companion
A man and a woman
whose dreams have gone out
and who no longer have
useless things
to tell each other.

34

لأنه لم يعد بيننا
حساء دافئ نتناوله
حديث فاتر نكرره .

Because between us
there is no warm soup to eat
and lukewarm words to repeat...

لأنه لم يعد بيننا
غير سرير
لا تنبت عليه إلا الطحالب
وليل لا يمحو
تعب النهار .

Because between us
there is no longer anything
except a bed
where only mushrooms grow
and night that does not erase
the weariness of the day...

لأنه لم يعد بيننا
سوى أطفال
نجهز لهم
أوهامنا
على طبق .

Because between us
there is nothing
but children
whom we serve
our delusions
on a plate...

لأنه أصبحنا
أكثر من الغرباء تهذيباً
وأقل من الأعداء إعجاباً .

Because we have become
more polite than strangers
and less than enemies
in our mutual admiration...

لأنه لم يعد بيننا
تلك الضحكات الشجيه
تلك اللمسات الصافية
وطعم
الغار والعسل
على شفاهنا .

Because between us
there are no longer
any unbridled laughs
and innocent touches
and the taste
of bay leaves and honey
on our lips...

لأنه لم يعد
بيننا .

Because between us
there is no longer...

35

أنا أعتذر ،
لأنني من حيث
لم أنتبه
هبت نسائمي
على أغصانك ،
فأوقعت
الزهرة الوحيدة التي
برعمت .

I apologise...
Unaware,
and unintentionally,
my breezes
shook your branches
and dropped
the only flower
you'd ever bloomed.

38

يثبت ذكرياته
بدبابيس رصاصية
على حيطان
غرفته ،
يجففها .
الصور
الورود
القبل
ورائحة الحب .
جميعها تنظر إليه
بعين الامتنان الحانية
لأنه جعلها
خالدة .
تقريباً خالدة ! .

He fixes his memories
with small lead pins
on the walls
of his room
to dry them.
Pictures
flowers
kisses
and the scent of love.
They all look at him
with eyes full of tender gratitude
because he made them
eternal,
almost eternal.

39

من وقت لوقت
يفتح الشبابيك
ومن وقت لآخر
يغلقها .
ظله يفضحه
من وراء ستائره
يذهب ويعود
يقترب ويبتعد .
يرفع صوت الحاكي
يعبئ بالموسيقى وحدته
موهماً الجيرة
بأن كل شيء كالمعتاد .
كنا نراه
يمر بسرعة ،
مطرق الرأس
حاملاً خبزه ؛
وعائداً
إلى حيث
لا أحد ينتظره .

From time to time
he opens the windows,
and every now and then
he closes them.
His silhouette betrays him
behind his curtains
as he comes and goes
his travels, far and near.
He turns up the radio
to fill his solitude with music,
deceiving the neighbours
that all is well.
We used to see him
hurrying past,
his head downcast,
carrying his bread
and returning
to where
no one waited for him.

40

ما كان يريدُ
أكثرَ من ذلك ،
بيتاً
وأطفالاً وزوجة
تحبه .
إلا أنه استيقظ يوماً
ليجدَ رُوحَه
قد هرمت .

ما كانت تريد
أكثر من ذلك ،
بيتاً وأطفالاً
وزوجاً يحبها .
إستيقظت
يوماً
لتجد
أن رُوحها
قد فتحت نافذة
وانطلقت .

He wanted
no more than this:
a house,
children and a wife
who loved him.
But he woke up one day
and found that his spirit
had grown old.

She wanted
no more than this:
a house, children
and a husband who loved her.
She woke up
one day
and found
that her spirit
had opened a window
and fled.

42

هذا المساء
سيخرجُ رجل ،
يبحث عن
فريسة
تُشبع سرُّ شهواته .

This evening
a man will go out
to look for
prey
to satisfy the secrets of his desires.

هذا المساء
ستخرج امرأة
تبحث عن
رجل يجعل منها
سيدةَ سريره .

This evening
a woman will go out
to look for
a man who will make her
mistress of his bed.

هذا المساء
ستجتمع الفريسة والصياد ،
سيختلطان ،
وربما ..
ربما
سيتبادلان الأدوار .

This evening
predator and prey will meet
and mix
and perhaps
perhaps
they will exchange roles.

44

لم يكن يخجل منها
بملابسه القطنية القديمة
وجواربه المثقوبة .
أمامها
كان يتعرى كما
تتعرى
حاجاتُ الحب ،
ليهبط
كالمَلك
على جسدها .

He felt no shame before her
in his old cotton clothes
and his torn socks.
He undressed,
the way the need for love
strips naked,
and descended
like an angel
upon her body.

45

لديه امرأتان ،
واحدة تنام في سريره
وواحدة تنام في سرير حلمه .

He has two women:
One sleeps in his bed,
the other sleeps
in the bed of his dreams.

لديه امرأتان تحبانه ،
واحدة تشيخ قربه
وواحدة تمنحه صباها
وتأفل .

He has two women who love him:
One ages beside him,
the other offers him her youth
then droops.

لديه إمرأتان
واحدة في قلب بيته
وواحدة في بيت قلبه .

He has two women:
one in the heart of his house,
one in the house of his heart.

At night
take her by the waist.
Kiss her throat like you kiss me
and hold in your hands
the fatigue of her exhausting day.
Tell her – for me –
that she is as beautiful
and desirable
as the day you met her.
Make love to her
the way you make love to me
until her silent birds
begin to chirp –
the woman
who is
my adversary.

مساءً
خذها من خصرها ،
قبّل عُنْقَها ، كما قبلتني ،
وامسح بيديك
تعبَ نهارها المُضْني .
قل لها – من أجلي –
مازالت جميلة
وشهية
كيوم عرفتها .
ضاجعها كما تحب أن تضاجعَني
حتى تغرّد
طيورُها الساكنة ،
المرأة
التي هي ...
غريمتي ! ؟

47

أتت كلها ،
برائحة سريرها
ومطبخها ،
بقبلات زوجها
المخبأة تحت قميصها ،
بسائله
الذي لا يزال ساخناً
في بطنها .

أتت ،
بتاريخها وأحلامها ،
بتجاعيدها
وابتسامتها المقشبه ،
بالزغب الذي يعشعش
على حافة وجنتيها ،
بأسنانها
التي علق عليها بقايا فطورها .

أتت بكل آلامي
المرأة التي يعيش معها رجلي .

She came whole,
with the smell of her bed
and her kitchen
with her husband's kisses
hidden under her blouse,
with his liquid
still hot
in her belly.

She came
with her history and her dreams,
with her wrinkles
and her reedy smile
and the fuzz adorning
the edges of her cheeks,
with her teeth
and the remains of her breakfast
between them.

She arrived with all my pains
the woman my man lives with.

48

هي التي
استباحت
رجلَ امرأة أخرى
فادخلته سرها
ومنحته شهوة جديدة
وجسداً .

هي الشريرة
التي يسمونها
آكلة الرجال
صادقة
اعطته قلبها
ليأكله .

She is the one
who seized
another woman's man,
and let him into her secret
and gave him a new pleasure
and a body.

She is the evil one
they call
a man-eater
who innocently
gives him her heart
to devour.

49

في شهقة اللحظة
إلتقينا .
عَبرتني ،
وعبرتك .
منحتني ألمي ،
ومنحتك فخرك .
ستذهب لتروي
أرضاً جديدة ،
وسأبقى أنا واجمة :
كيف
تشابكت أيدينا .

In the heaving of a moment
we met.
You crossed me
and I traversed you.
You gave me my pain
and I gave you your pride.
You will go to water
a new earth,
and I will remain ponderous:
How did
our hands get entangled?

على الفراش
بقعة حمراء
مبللة بدموع شهوة عذراء
تُحب لأوّل مرة
وتغْتسل بماء الحياة الأبدي .
ذلك العرق
الساخن
وروائحه الغريبة
التي تنبثق
من جسدين
يحتفلان
بموت الرغبة .

On the bed,
a red spot
stained with the tears of a virgin desire.
She loves for the first time
and bathes in the eternal water of life –
that hot
sweat
and its strange scents
emanating
from two bodies
celebrating
the death of desire.

52

جاءني
متخفياً في جسد رجل
فلم آبَهْ به .
قال لي
افتحي
فأنا الروح القدس .
وخوفاً من المعصية
تركته يقبلني ،
عرّى
بنظراته
نهديَّ الخجولين ؛
حولني لامرأة جميلة .
ثم نفخَ في جسدي رُوحَه
هادراً
رعداً وصواعقَ .
آمنت .

He came to me
disguised in the body of a man
and I ignored him.
He said:
Open up
I am the holy spirit.
I feared disobeying him
so I let him kiss me.
He uncovered
my shy breasts
with his gaze
and turned me into
a beautiful woman.
Then he blew his spirit into my body,
rumbling thunder and lightning.
And I believed.

53

علمها أن
تتفتح
كزهرة رمّان حمراء ،
أن تُنصتَ
لوشوشاَت جسدها ،
وأن تصرخ ،
بدل أن
تَئد آهاتها ،
وهي
تسقط
كورقة مرتعشة .

He taught her
to open up
like a pomegranate blossom,
and to listen
to the whispers of her body,
and to scream out
instead
of muffling her sighs
as she
fell
like a trembling leaf.

57

كان عليك
ألا تمسك بيديّ ،
لتترك لهما
الحلم بلمسك .

You should not
have touched my hand
and left it dreaming
of your touch.

كان عليك
ألا تقبّل شفتيّ ،
لتجعلهما
تحترقان للثمك .

You should not
have kissed my lips
and left them burning
for your muffling caress.

كان عليك
أن تصمت ،
كي لا أتوقف عن
الأمل .

You should have
remained quiet
so that I would not stop
hoping.

59

كنت أسير على الصراط
المستقيم
عندما اعترضت طريقي
اختل توازني
إلا أنني
لم أقع.

I was on the straight
path
when you blocked my way.
I stumbled
but I did not
fall.

60

بفاكهتي الجميلة
أضيء
الطريق المؤدي إليّ .

With my delicious fruit
I light
the way leading to me.

طيورك الغبية
تحب
الخبز اليابس .

Your stupid birds
prefer
old bread.

62

سأغمض عينيّ ،
ولن أقوم بحراسة
معبدك .
هذه المرة
سأدع
الإله العربيد
يهرب حافياً .

I will close my eyes
and stop guarding
your temple.
This time
I will let
the mischievous god
escape barefoot.

63

باركني حرة
واصبر
على تمنعي .
اقترب عندما
أدعوك ،
وعندما
أهملك ،
تعلم انتظاري .
أقبلني لغيرك
وتعلم الحب .

Bless me with freedom
and be patient
with my fussing.
Come closer when
I invite you,
and when I neglect you,
learn to wait.
Desire me for someone
other than yourself
and learn to love.

64

كانت تأتيه
لتهبه
مساماتها
وأناملها
المزينةَ بالكَرَز
يأكلها بنهم .

She set out
to offer him
her pores
and her nails
adorned with cherries
which he ate
ravenously.

كانت تذهب
وسلّةُ قلبها
فارغة .

She left
with the basket
of her heart
emptied out.

65

يتكوّرُ صدري
بشوق الرغبة ،
رغيفاً ساخناً
تقضمه
أسنانُ
عبثِك .

My chest swells
with a longing for lust,
a hot loaf of bread
bitten
by the teeth
of your folly.

66

لن آتي
إلى حيث ينتظرني ،
في المكان القريب الذي لا أعرفه .

I will not go
to the place where he waits for me,
the nearby place I know well.

ها أنا أغسل شعري
فيما إذا أراد أن يداعبَه ،
وأضع الرائحة التي يحب
فيما إذا اقترب لِيَضُمَّني .

Here I am washing my hair,
in case he wanted to caress it,
and putting on the perfume he loves
in case he comes close to embrace me.

لن آتي
إلى حيث ينتظرني ،
سأربط قدميَّ
وستنتابُني الحمَّى .

I will not go
to the place where he waits.
I will bind my feet,
and a fever will strike me.

ها أنا ألبس معطفي وأخرج :
خروفٌ صغير
ذاهب للمذبح .

Here I am putting on my coat and leaving:
a lamb
heading for slaughter.

68

كل مساءات أيامه
كان يخطط
رحيلها
فيتألم .

Every night
he planned
her departure
and it pained him.

كل صباحات أيامه
كان يدخلها حجره
فيسعد برؤيتها
تدفئه بحبها .

Every morning
he placed her in her hovel,
and it pleased him to see her
warm him with her love.

كان ينتظر المناسبة
ليقول لها ارحلي ،
وفي كل مناسبه
لا يجد المناسبه .
جائعه وهو الوليمه
عارية وهو ثيابها .

He waited for the right time
to tell her to leave.
But every time
he could not find the time.
She was starving and he was her feast;
she was naked and he was her clothes.

ينساها
فهي لا تأخذ مكاناً ،
وعندما يتذكرها
يجدها تحت إبطه ؛
يقتلها
فيرى قدمها
في حذائه
وبطنها الحار
على جسده .

When he forgot her
she seemed to disappear,
and when he remembered her
he found her nosing his armpit.
He killed her
then saw her feet
in his shoes,
and her hot belly
resting against his side.

كان يجد نفسه
جميلاً في سريرها
وهي تبعثر برفق
حاجبيه المرتبين ،
وتمسح بشعرها
غبار صدره .

He found himself
beautiful in her bed
as she softly dishevelled
his well-groomed eyebrows,
and as she swept with her hair
the dust off his chest.

قضى عمره
يفكر
كيف لرجل مثله
أن يترك
امرأة
مثلها .

He spent his life
thinking
how a man like him
could leave
a woman
like her.

69

لم تنفع
فساتيني
التي اشتريتها جديدة ،
ولا النظرات
الدافئة
التي كنت أرمقه بها .
لم تنفع كلمات الحب ،
ولا نصائح أوفيد .
لا شعري الأسود الطويل
ولا طراوة جلدي اللامع .
لم تنفع لهفتي
ولا عذوبتي
لا إبتساماتي ولا دموعي
أن تطوّع
قلب الحب
القاسي .

The new dresses
I bought
did not help
or the warm
looks
I tossed him.
My tender words did not help,
nor Ovid's counsel.
Not even my long black hair
or my glowing soft skin.
My lust did not help,
nor my sweetness,
nor my smiles and tears,
to soften
the hard heart
of love.

43

70

عصفورٌ A sparrow
يموت في يدي ،   dies in my hands.
لم يعد It is no longer
دافئاً وطرّياً ،   warm and soft.
لا هواجس No thoughts
تسكنه   occupy it now,
ولا أحلام ،   and no dreams.
يموت كيوم بلا حب . It dies like a day without love.

71

حضنت I embraced
جذعك . your trunk,
هززته I shook it
ألماً ، with pain,
فانهمرت and drops of your dew
قطرات نداك fell into
على جرحي . my wound.

44

72

لن يكون
أَلَمُكَ
أكثرَ من وخزة إبرة
وأنا أدير ظهري .
سيكون ألمي
أحمرَ
كَهَصْرِ كَرَزة ناضجةٍ
على بلاطٍ
أبيض ،
وأنا أراقب
إبتسامةَ الخلاص
عَلى طرف فمك .

Your pain
was not
more than a pin prick.
But as I turn around me
my pain
will be red
like a ripe cherry mashed
on a white
tile
when I see a smile
of relief
on the side of your mouth.

but not Haiku

73

الأفعى ستموت
عندما
ستلسعني
ستذوق
ألمي .

The serpent will die
when
it bites me
and tastes
my pain.

74

تجلوها
كشمس لعيني سجين .
تبسطها
كزُهور البنفسج
تحت حذاء عسكري .
تمنحها
كريمة كَثَدْي أمٍ .
تفتتها كالخبز
لطيور جائعة ...

ماذا ينفع
أن تعري الروحَ هكذا
أمام
من لا يرى .

You reveal it
like the sun to a prisoner's eyes.
You spread it
like narcissus flowers
before soldiers' boots.
You offer it
generously like mother's breast.
You crumble it like bread
for hungry birds...

What good does it do
to undress the soul this way
before one
who cannot see?

75

حب آخر يموت ؛
سترتبه المرأة بخنوع
في خزانة ذكرياتها
المليئة
بطيور أحلامها
المحنطة .

Another love dies:
Submissively the woman
will place it
in the wardrobe of her memories
filled
with the embalmed birds
of her dreams.

77

لملم بيديك
باقة
خصري الطرية
من على السرير
المليء بأشلاء
الضحايا ...

Gather in your hands
the bouquet
of my soft waist
from a bed
full of the victims'
severed limbs.

80

ماذا فعلت بغيابك ؟
غيَّرت ماء حوض السمكة الحمراء ،
سقيت النبتة الصغيرة ،
رتّبت أنفاسي ،
وبدأت أنسجُ
كَنزَة الصوف !

What did I do in your absence?
I changed the water
in the goldfish bowl,
I watered the small plant,
I regulated my breathing
and began knitting
the woollen sweater.

82

كالكتب المحرَّمة
أخفيك تحت وسادتي .
تنامُ الأضواء
تنام الأصوات
فأخرِجُك
وأبدأ
بالتهامِك .

I hide you under my pillow
like a forbidden book.
The lights sleep
and the sounds sleep.
Then I take you out
and begin
devouring you.

83

لا تنظر إلى هذه الكدمة
الزرقاء ،
ولا إلى الجرح
الذي يعلو قلبي .
لا تنظر
إلى التجاعيد التي بدأت تحفر
حول عيني ،
ولا إلى الشعرات البيضاء
التي تنبت في رأسي .
فقط
لرُوحي ..

روحي
عشبُ آذارَ الجديد .

Don't look at the blue
bruise
or the wound
above my heart.
Don't look
at the wrinkles that began to scratch
the edges of my eyes,
or at the white hairs
sprouting from my head.
Look only
to my soul,
my soul
the new grass of March.

85

سلطان النوم
المستبد
يسرقك مني .

وحيدة قربك ،
أعد النجوم المعلقة على أهدابك
وأجس
نبض وقتي المحتضر
في فمي بقايا كلمات
وفي أصابعي رغبة
لا تستكين ..

Sleep,
that merciless tyrant,
snatches you from me.

Alone beside you
I count the stars suspended from
your eyelashes
and take the pulse
of my dying time –
word scraps in my mouth,
and in my fingers
an unstoppable urge.

87

عندما تخرج
من حذائك
وتتركه
وحيداً
على عتبة الباب
أو تحت السرير
يحتله الضجر
وأقدام الانتظار الباردة .

When you take off
your shoes
and leave them
lonely
on the doorstep
or under the bed
they are filled by boredom
and the cold feet of waiting.

90

معلقة
كذرات الهواء
على معطفك .
كنقطة ماء على حافة
ذقنك .
كعنكبوت بين الفراغ
والفراغ .
كمصير
بين شفتي الله .

Suspended
like air particles
on your coat
like a drop of water
on the tip
of your chin.
Like a spider between emptiness
                and emptiness.
like a destiny
between God's lips.

91

مللت البقاء
على هامشك
في مسوداتك
على أدراجك
أمام أبوابك .
أين
فسيح جنانك ؟ ! ؟

I am bored with being
in your margins,
in your notebooks,
in your traces,
before your doors.
Where
are the wide spans of your heavens?

92

تعال عارياً
لألبسك
جسدك
الذي استعاره خيالي .

Come naked
that I may dress you again
with your body
which my imagination
has borrowed.

93

نظرت إلى مرآتي
فرأيت
امرأة
مليئة بالرضى
ذات عيون مضيئة
وخبث لذيذ

حسدتها .

I looked into my mirror
and saw
a woman / MAN
filled with contentment
and with bright eyes
and delicious mischief,

and I envied her / HIM

GOOD

95

قولوا للريح
أن تهدأ
فأنا لا أحب الريح .
إنها قادرة
كامرأة غيور
على أن تنبش شعري
وأنا ذاهبة
لأقابل
الذي ينتظرني .

Tell the wind
to calm,
for I don't love the wind.
It can
like a jealous woman
riffle through my hair
as I go out
to meet
the one who waits for me.

قولوا للمطر
أن يتوقف
فأنا لا أُحِبّ
المطر .
إنه قادر
كزوج غيور
على أن يبلل ثيابي
وحذائي الجديد ،
وأنا أنتظر
ذلك الذي
لم
يأت .

Tell the rain
to stop,
for I don't love
the rain.
It can
like a jealous husband
drench my clothes
and my new shoes
as I wait
for the one
who has yet
to arrive.

96

لحسن الحظ
لديّ قلم
وورقة
يخففان
وطأة انتظارك ،
وإن لم ...
سآكل أظافري
وأركل بعصبية
النمل
الذي بدأ يتسلق ساقي .

Fortunately
I have pen and paper
    to lighten
    the pain of waiting for you.
    If not…
I would gnaw at my fingers
and nervously kick
at the ants
that have begun to climb
my trunk.

VERY, VERY GOOD

97

أعطني كذباتك
أغسلها
ادخلها براءة قلبي
أجعلها حقائق .

Give me your lies.
I will wash them
and tuck them in
the innocence of my heart
to make them facts.

98

تختلف عنهم كثيراً ...
علامتك الفارقة
قبلتي
على
فمك .

You are very different from them...
Your distinction:
My kiss
is on
your mouth.

100

لم يكن ذَنْبك
لم يكن ذنبي .
هي الريح
أوْقَعت
مشمشةً شهوتي
الناضجة .

It was not your fault.
It was not my fault.
It was the wind
that brought down
the ripe apricot
of my desire.

102

أنا وفرحي
ننتظر
رفيفَ خطواتِك .

My happiness and I
await
the flutter of your steps.

103

كحبات ملح
كانوا يلمعون
ثم ذابوا .
هكذا رحلوا
هؤلاء الرجال
الذين لم يحبوني .

Like grains of salt
they shone
then melted.
This is how they disappeared,
those men
who did not love me.

105

أنا في البرد
والعتمه ،
لماذا
لا تفتح لي
بابَ قميصِك .

I am out in the cold,
in the dark.
Why
don't you open the door
of your shirt to me?

FROM

I Look to You

Andhur Elaik

(2000)

1

لنا وجوهٌ
نحملُها على اكتافِنا
على بطاقاتِ هوياتِنا
في صُوَرِنا التذكارية

We have faces
we carry on our shoulders,
on our identity cards
and family pictures.

لنا وجوهٌ
نمزِّقُها نحفظُها
نخبِّئُها نكشفُها
نألفُها نُنْكِرُها
نحبُّها
ونكرهُها

We have faces
we shred and keep,
hide and reveal,
faces we become accustomed to
and shun,
that we love
and hate.

لنا وجوهٌ
نعرِفُها..
نقولُ: نعرفُها ؟

We have faces
we recognise…
And we say: recognise?

2

«هنالكَ
دائماً من يشبُهنا
في مكانٍ ما»
قالتِ العاهرةُ الصغيرةُ
وهيَ تبتسمُ بثقةٍ
ناظرةً إلى النافذةِ
وكأنها تَرَى
حُلْمَها
شجرةً موفورةَ
الثمارْ..

'There's always
someone who resembles us
somewhere in the world,'
said the little prostitute
smiling with assurance,
looking at the window
as if she saw
her dream
shaped like a tree
laden with fruit.

59

3

الرُّمَّانةُ
المحتَفِظةُ بأسرارِ
لآلئها
لا تزالُ تنتَظِرُ
أن تخلعَ
قِشرتَها اللامعة..

العطشُ موعودٌ
بسائلٍ
طيِّبْ..

The pomegranate
guarding the secrets
of her pearls
still waits
for her shiny skin
to be disrobed.

Thirst is promised
a sweet
liquid.

4

اُستطيعُ أن أُميِّزَها
مِنْ بينِ كلَّ
القبلاتِ
تلكَ التي تطبُعُها الرغْبَة.

اُستطيعُ أن أعرِفَها
مِنْ كلَّ
الرغباتِ
تلكَ
التي يؤجِّجُها
الحُبَّ..

I can tell it apart
from all
the kisses
desire has stamped on me.

I can recognise it
among all
the desires
that
love
emblazons.

5

أيّ
جُرمٍ جميلٍ
اقترفتُ؟

What
beautiful crime
have I committed?

تمتّعتُ
بجسَدٍ
أهداني
نهراً مُسكراً
وانتفاضةَ حياةٍ..

I enjoyed
a body
that gave me
a soporific river
and an upheaval of life.

6

ماذا بوسعها أنْ تفعلَ
أمامَ موجةٍ عارمةٍ كهذِهِ
في حرٍّ كهذا؟

What could she have done
in a heat-wave like this
on a hot day like this one?

زَبَدُ البحرِ
لامسَ بطنَ قَدَمِها
فانتابَها
شعورٌ من القشعريرةِ
أنساها
الصلاةَ..

Sea foam
touched the arch of her foot
and she was swallowed
by a wave of trembling
that made her forget
her prayers.

7

ماذا أسمعُ؟	What do I hear?
تفتُّحَ وردةٍ	A rose opening
وصهيلَ جَوَادٍ..	and a horse neighing...

ماذا أرى؟	What do I see?
سُحْباً	Clouds
تتوهَّجُ في حُضْني	gleaming in my lap
ومَطَراً	and rain
يَهْطُلُ..	pouring...

8

قالت: نَعَمْ	She said: Yes
التهمْتُهُ..	I devoured him...
كنتُ جائعةً	I was hungry
كَرَجُلٍ..	like a man...

وكَرَجُلٍ	And like a man
طَرَحْتُهُ رغْبَتي	I splayed him across my desires
مُزْدَهِرةً بذكورَتِها..	blossoming with masculinity.

9

اعْدُو اركُضُ اتمهَّلُ اصعَدُ اهبِطُ
ادنو ابتعدُ اصرخُ
ائنُّ الهَثُ اصْمُتُ اَضِيعُ اتواجدُ اعصِفُ امُد
ابكي اضْحَكْ..

امرأةٌ في عُرْسِ شهوَتِها
تضجُّ بملائكةِ رَجُل..

I run   jog   I tarry   rise
    and descend
I come   close   move away
    I scream
I moan   pant   fall quiet
    disappear   and become
I storm   I rain
I weep   I laugh

A woman in the feast of her ecstasy
thronged by a man's host of angels.

10

كفقيرٍ يأكُلُ
حتّى التُّخمةِ
خوفاً من يومٍ
لا طعامَ فيهِ

انظرُ إليكَ
في حُضْني..

Like a destitute
overstuffing himself
dreading a day
without food

I look to you
in my lap.

11

اُفَتِّشُ عَنْ قِطَعِ
ثِيابي
لِتُلْبِسَني.

I search for pieces
of my clothes
to wear me.

اَلمِلمُ بصمْتٍ
دموعَ
اللَّذة..

I gather in silence
tears
of pleasure.

اتخلَّصُ مِن براهينَ مُرُودي
تاركةً إِلِكَ
غائباً عن الوعي لرحيلي
قتيلًا طرِيًا
كأنَّكَ نائِمْ..

I erase all evidence of my arrival
leaving you
unconscious of my departure.
A tender corpse
as if you were asleep.

13

نَسْمةَ هواءٍ
أَنسلُّ بينَ
شَفَتَي بابِكَ
مثلَ نَفَسٍ أخيرٍ
ولا تَتشبَّثُ بي..

A breeze,
I slip in
between the lips of your door
like a last breath
and you do not cling to me.

14

لا تَكُنْ فاتِراً
فأتَقيَّؤُكَ..

Don't be so stale
that I have to vomit you.

إشتَعِلْ
مِثْلَ
جَمرةٍ
مِثْلَ
احتكاكِ غُصْنَينِ
تَوَهَّجْ..

Spark up
like
an ember.
Like
the rubbing of two branches
flame up!

هكذا أُحِبُّ
الحياةَ
في مَضْجَعي..

That's how I love
life
in my bower.

ستَسْكُنُكَ
رائِحتي..
وعندما ستَتعرَّى
ستَعْبَقُ
مُتَّهمةً إيّاكَ
بخيانتي..

My scent will
invade you,
and when you undress
it will spread and spread
accusing you
of betraying me.

16

كلُّ ما أملِكُ
افرُشُهُ
كعُشبٍ..

All that I own
I spread around me
like grass.

أصابعُكَ تُحرّرُني
طليقةً أُصبحُ
كريحٍ..

Your fingers release me,
and free I become
like a gust of wind.

17

الرَّغَباتُ
عواصفُ
تَرتَطِمُ بحاجزٍ
(ممنوع المرور)

Desires are
storms
that crash against a barrier
(No Through Road).

طريقُكَ
لا يَمُرُّ في شارعي..

Your path
does not run along my street.

19

قالتْ سينامُ العنكبوتُ
بينَ خيطانِهِ
مصائرُ الفراشاتِ الضالَّة.

She said the spider will sleep –
in his web
will be
the destinies of wayward moths.

سيتغذَّى
بجَهْلِها.

He will feed
on their ignorance.

20

أعرفُ أنَّهُ
لم يكُنْ عَلَيَّ
أنْ أدعَهُ
يكشِفُ عن نَهدَيَّ
كنتُ أُريدُ
فَقَطْ
أنْ أُرِيَهُ
أَنَّني امرأة..

I know
I shouldn't have
let him
uncover my breasts.
I only
wanted
to show him
I'm a woman.

أعرفُ أنَّهُ
لم يكُنْ عَلَيَّ
أنْ أتركَهُ يتعرَّى
كانَ
يُريدُ
أن يريَني أنَّهُ
رجُلٌ
فَقَطْ..

I know
I shouldn't
have let him
undress.
He only
wanted
to show me
he's
a man.

67

21

بِكَثِيرٍ مِنَ الحنانِ
إكشِفْ اغطِيَتَها
برفقٍ
ضَعْ اصابِعَكَ
على جَسَدِها.

With great affection,
lift her covers,
and with tenderness
place your fingers
on her body.

امرأةٌ سهلةٌ؟
ربَّما
امرأةٌ مهجورةٌ؟
حتماً..

An easy woman?
Perhaps...
An abandoned woman?
Certainly...

22

... وكَشَفَ لي
عُرْيَهُ
جوعَ جَسَدِهِ
وجوعَ روحِهِ
وما تركَ العُمْرُ
مِنْ بُثورٍ
وجُروحٍ
مِنْ جَمَالٍ وقُبح..

... and he showed
his nakedness,
the hunger of his body,
and the hunger of his soul
and what time had imprinted
in scabs
and wounds
in beauty and ugliness.

غَطَّيتُهُ
بلِحافِ الرَغْبَة..

I wrapped him
in the blanket of desire.

23

قالت: لِنَتَصَنَّع الحُبَّ
في شِبهِ سريرٍ
يَضُمُّ
شِبهَ رَجُلٍ
شِبهَ امرأةٍ

بعواطفَ
شِبهِ حقيقيةٍ
فارشِينَ حَولَنا
ورودًا شِبهَ مَيِّتةٍ
لكي لا تموتُ..

She said,
'Let's pretend to make love
in a pretend-bed
that includes
a pretend-man
a pretend-woman

with emotions
that are almost real
spreading around us
almost-dead flowers
so that they would not die.'

24

جِلدُكَ
يَجِفُّ
ينضُبُ
ينشَفُ
يقحَلُ
يَتَشَقَّقُ..
جِلدُكَ
يُؤلِمُكَ..

عَرَقي لم يَهطُلْ عليه..

Your skin
dries
itches
flakes
blisters
inflames
cracks up.
Your skin
hurts you.

My sweat has not poured upon it.

27

اقيسُ مدى استطاعتي
خيانتَكَ
بـأنْ اتخيَّلَكَ
في حُضْنِ امرأةٍ أُخرى..

I measure my ability
to betray you
by imagining you
in another woman's embrace.

فأتوبُ
واستغفرُكَ..

Then I repent
and seek your mercy.

28

أرجوكَ
أن تأتيَ..

I beg you…
come…

لقدْ طلبتُ فنجانَ القهوةِ
وخوفاً أنْ
أتأخَّرَ
نسيتُ
مِحفظةَ نقودي..

I've ordered a cup of coffee
and fearing that
I'd be late
I forgot
my purse.

29

يسيلُ عليها لعابُ الآلهةِ
وَهيَ
تَنْتَظِرْ..

The gods' mouths
will drool
on her
as she
waits.

30

لا بُدَّ
أنّكَ نسيتَ
أوراقَكَ
فَعُدتَ على أعقابِكَ..

You must have
forgotten
your papers
and returned to retrieve them.

أو أنَّ
صديقًا اتّصلَ
ثمَّ راحَ يُثرثِرْ
وأنتَ تهمُّ بالخروجْ..

Or
a friend must have called
and began to chatter
as you were about to leave.

أو لا بُدَّ
أنّكَ تنتظِرُني
في مقهىً آخَرْ..

Or you must
be waiting for me
in another café.

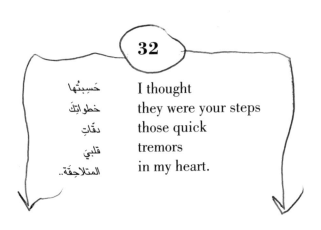

32

حَسِبتُها
خطواتِكَ
دقّاتِ
قلبِيَ
المتلاحِقَة..

I thought
they were your steps
those quick
tremors
in my heart.

33

قالَت: رُبَّما
ما زالَ الحُبُّ
يَنْتَظِرُ..

She said, 'Perhaps
love is still
waiting.'

مِظلَّةٌ تَحْتَ كُرسِيٍّ
كتابٌ على مقعدٍ
امرأةٌ تَحْسَبُ أنَّهُ
سيأتي..

An umbrella under a chair,
a book on another.
A woman who thinks it will
come.

35

لا...
ليسَ بابُكَ
الذي أَطرُقُ
والذي
أَسمَعُ
خَلْفَهُ
انفاسًا
والذي
رَغْمَ انكسارِ مِصرَاعَيْهِ
لا يُفْتَحُ..

No...
It's not your door
I'm knocking on.
It's not the one
behind which
I hear
breathing.
It's not the one
broken off its hinges
which still refuses
to open.

36

يَعرفُ
رائحةَ إِبطي
مسامُّ جِلدي
طَعْمَ لُعابي..

رَجُلٌ مَنَحَني ماءَهُ
ومنَحْتُهُ مائي..

رَجُلٌ خانَ
ذاكرَتَهُ..

He knows
the scent of my armpits,
the pores of my skin,
the taste of my saliva.

A man who gave me
his water
and whom I gave
my water.

A man who betrayed
his own memory.

37

ستهجُرُني؟
إذنْ
مَنْ سيرى
فُستانَ عُرِيْ
الذي أبدو فيهِ
حَقًّا
جميلة؟

You'll abandon me?
Who will
then see
the attire of my nakedness
in which I appear
truly
beautiful?

39

سيقتَفي أَثَرَكَ
خَيَالي
إِن ذهبتَ
خطوةً خطوةً
اَمامَكَ
خطوةً خطوةً
خلفَك..

My shadow
will follow your traces
step by step
as you go
forward,
and step by step
as you go
back.

كالذَّنبِ
اَشدُّني إليكَ
ولا اُريدُ الخَلاصْ..

Like sin
I cling to you
never desiring salvation.

40

اَمامَ صَدرِكَ
اَربُضُ
اُلمِلمُ
زَفيرَكَ
اَخبِّئُهُ ليومِ اختناقي..

By your bed
I crouch
and gather
your exhales
for the day of my asphyxiation.

43

رَجُلٌ لَه فَمٌ
ولا يتكَلَّمُ
شَفَتانِ
ولا يُقَبِّلُ..

A man who has a mouth
but does not speak
has lips
but does not kiss.

رَجُلٌ لَه أَنْفٌ
ولا يَشُمُّ
له اذنانِ ولا يَسْمَعْ..
رَجُلٌ له
عينانِ حزينتانِ
وذراعانِ طويلتانِ
لا تعرفانِ العِناقْ..

A man who has a nose
but does not smell
has ears but does not hear.
A man who has
sad eyes
and long arms
but does not know
how to embrace.

رَجُلُ القَشِّ
خَدَعَ
عصافيري..

A scarecrow
has tricked
my sparrows.

44

سيُثْقِلُ ضِلْعَهُ
هبوبُ أنْفاسِها..

His ribs will be burdened
by her breathing.

سيضيقُ سريرُهُ
الحائطُ أمامَهُ
وهيَ خلْفَهُ..

His bed will grow small –
the wall before him
and her body behind him.

ستتذمَّرُ قدماهُ
فلمْ يَعُدْ لهما فُسْحَة..

His feet will grumble –
nowhere for them to go.

قليلًا وترحَلُ
سيتمطَّى بطولِ ذراعيهِ
وسيفلِشُ صُرَّةَ أضلاعِهِ
مُدركًا حينَها
أنَّ الحائطَ ما بَرِحَ أمامَهُ
وخلْفَهُ
هاويةُ
فراغِها..

A little while and she'll be gone.
He will stretch the length of his arms' span.
He will empty out the bundle of his ribs
and then realise
the wall is no longer before him,
and behind him
there is the abyss
of her absence.

45

ليسَ من السُّكَّرِ
والعَسَلْ..

Not of sugar
or honey…

مصنوعٌ مِنَ التَعَبِ
واللهموم
مِنَ الذكرياتِ
والاحلامِ
مِنَ القسوةِ
والجَفافِ
مِنَ العُشبِ والماءِ
مجبولٌ بالوهمِ
والخوفْ..

He's made of fatigue
                    worries,
memories
            and dreams,
hardship
            and drought,
of grass and water,
wound up in illusions
and terrors.

46

قلبٌ مثقوبٌ
برصاصاتِ الخيبةِ المُتَتالِيَة..

A heart punctured
by consecutive bullets of failure.

52

إنه يَئِنْ
يتوجَّعُ
أَيِّلٌ يُحْتَضَرْ..

He is moaning
in pain,
a deer breathing his last.

كَمْ رصاصةً بقيَ؟
وَكَمْ
من رحْمَة..

How many bullets are left?
How much
mercy?

77

53

ماذا يفعلُ جَوادٌ
بعُنُقٍ جميلٍ
مكسورْ؟

What does a horse do
with a beautiful broken
neck?

54

كان مُخْتَفياً
عندما فجأةً
عادَ واحتلَّ غُرفةَ الجلوسْ..

He was hiding,
then suddenly
he returned and took over the living-room.

صَعَدَ من القبو
تمدَّدَ على الأريكةِ
غيَّرَ محطَّةَ التِلفزيون
غيَّرَ محطَّةَ الراديو
ثمَّ...
ثمَّ راحَ يتمشَّى بسروالِهِ الداخليِّ
كأنَّهُ في بيتِهِ

He climbed from the basement
and stretched out on the sofa.
He changed the TV channel,
changed the radio station,
then
began to pace in his underwear
as if he were in his own house.

تعرَّى..
ولم تكُن ترى
سوى
رَجُلٍ نَسِيَتْهُ..

He undressed
and she saw nothing
except
a man she'd forgotten.

56

ثِيابٌ قَديمةٌ
تَملأُ خِزانتَها
واطفالٌ يأتونَ
مساءً
بِضجيجٍ
ونتائجَ ضَعيفَة..

Old clothes
fill her wardrobe,
and children
come
in the evening
with a loud din
and low test scores.

زوجٌ هَجَرَها
وعشيقٌ لم يعُدْ لَدَيهِ
وقتْ..

A husband who abandoned her,
and a lover who no longer has
the time.

57

في الشارعِ المؤدّي
إلى منزلِها
صالونُها مضيءٌ
طيفُها
يتأرجَحُ
كقنديلْ..
تريدُ من اللهِ
أن يلوّحَ لها بِمِرْوَحةِ نسائِمِهِ
أو يُبَلْسِمَ بأنفاسِهِ
حُروقَها
كأمٍّ حَنونْ..

On the street
to her house
her living room appears lit
and her silhouette
swings
like a lantern...
She wants God
to wave at her
with the fan of his breezes
or to balm her burns
with his breath
like a kind mother.

59

الصمتُ يحضُنُ
المنزلَ المُعْتِمَ
كعشيقٍ جديدٍ..

Silence enfolds
the dark house
like a new lover.

المرأةُ في السريرِ الكبيرِ
تنتظرُ
شبهَ يائسةٍ
مجيءَ النُعاسِ
الذي هَجَرَها
أيضاً..

The woman in the large bed
waits
almost desperate
for the coming of sleep
which too
has abandoned her.

62

قالت: بقيَ
جدارٌ
ببصَماتٍ سوداءَ
وظلالٍ
ينتظرُ عِنايتي..

She said, 'There remains
a wall
with black fingerprints
and shadows
that needs my care...

وحدَها الجدرانُ
لا تُبارحُ.
بل تزدادُ
التِصَاقاً بي..

Only walls
stay put.
Rather they seem to be leaning
toward me.'

63

نَسِيتَ
أنَّها أُنثى

She forgot
she was a female,

تلكَ التي نظرتْ
إلى حُزنِها
كَفُقاعاتِ صابونٍ
وتلَهَّيْتَ باظافِرِكَ
وَهِيَ
تَغْرَقُ..

she who looked
at her sadness
as if it were bubbles,
and distracted herself
with his fingernails
as she
drowned.

65

البيتُ مُتْعَبٌ
غُرَفُهُ العُليا
لم تَعُدْ مأهولةً..
البيتُ يُعاني الصمتْ..

في الجهةِ الشِماليّةِ
شَقٌّ
تأتي منهُ العواصفُ
وخيوطُ الماءِ المُخْضَرّةْ..

مشلولٌ
لا يستطيعُ الركضَ
ولا الذهابَ إلى حيثُ يُحِبُّ

كَمْ كانَ يحلُمُ بسعاداتٍ بسيطةٍ
كَمْ توخّى الجَمَالَ
وكَمْ حَزِنَ لرؤيةِ جُدرانِهِ تتقشّرُ
وصُفرةُ الدخانِ والزَمَنِ
تعتلي بَياضَه..

The house is tired,
its upper rooms
no longer lived in.
The house throbs with silence.

In the north corner
a crack
where storms blow in
and threads of green water flow.

Crippled
it can't run
or go where it wishes.

How it dreamt of small happinesses,
how it aspired to beauty,
how sad it was to see its walls peel
and the yellowness of smoke and time
crawling up its whiteness!

68

نافذةٌ	A window
نِصفُ مفتوحةٍ	half open
نِصفُ مُغلَقةٍ	half closed.
نافذةٌ	A window
نِصفُ مغطّاةٍ	half covered
نِصفُ مكشوفةٍ	half uncovered.
نافذةٌ	A window
نِصفُ مُضيئةٍ	half lit
نِصفُ مُعْتِمةٍ	half dark
تُطلُّ على حائطٍ	facing a wall
تُطلُّ على حديقةٍ	facing a garden
على شارعٍ	a street
على عُشْبٍ	grass
على إسفلتٍ	asphalt
على اَسْوَدَ	facing black
على أَخْضَرْ..	facing green.

The window of love.

نافذةُ الحُبِّ..

69

خَيالانِ
لو تمعّنتَ جيّداً
لميّزْتَ ذِراعينِ
ثُمَّ نَهدينِ..

Two apparitions —
if you looked closer
you'd notice two arms
and two breasts.

امرأةٌ مُنهَمكةٌ حتى الغيابِ
في خُضْنِها رأْسُهُ
تعجُنهُ تُكتّلُهُ، تُدوّرُهُ، تَلُفُّهُ..
يداهُ تعرّشانِ على جِذعِها.

A woman, busy and absent-minded.
His head is on her chest.
She kneads it, moulds it,
she turns it, and wraps it
while his hands rest on her trunk.

تدورُ حولَهُ
يدورُ حولَها
تركعُ أمامَهُ
يركعُ أمامها
تغسِلُهُ
ويغسِلُها
تهيّئُهُ
يُهيّئُها..

She swivels around him.
He swivels around her.
She bends before him.
He bends before her.
She washes him.
and he washes her.
She prepares him
and he prepares her.

في حَمّامِ البيتِ المقابِلْ..

In the bathroom
of the house opposite…

70

البَعُوضةُ
وليستْ عودةُ زوجِها
ما أيقظَ
آلامَها
بعدَ مُنْتَصفِ الليل..

A mosquito,
not her husband's return,
is what awakened
her pains
after midnight…

عَرَفَتْ هذا
من البَصَماتِ الحمراءِ
الملتهبة
التي وَجَدَتْها
على خَدّها..

She became aware of this
from the red fingerprints
she found
flaring
on her cheek…

71

لماذا نَسيتَ
أن تُطفئَ
قبلَ أن تنامَ
مِصباحَ
رَغْبتي المتوهّجَ؟

Before you fell asleep
why did you forget
to switch off
the lamp
of my burning desires?

تَرَكْتَني
مُضيئةً
لطيورٍ شَرِسَة..

You left me,
a bright and radiant target
for birds of prey.

73

قالت: لماذا لا يأتونَ
محمّلينَ بسعادتِهِمْ
ونَجاحِ أطفالِهِمْ
ذكرياتِهِمْ
ومشاريعِهِمْ
يُشاركوننَي
عَشائي !؟

She said, 'Why don't they come
bearing their happiness
and the successes of their children,
their memories,
their plans,
and share a meal
with me?'

74

بيتُ أصدقائي
قريبٌ
وبيتي
بعيدٌ بعيدْ...

My friends' house
is close,
and my house
far, far away.

75

ورَّثَتْ أطفالَها
أُمّاً تَحْلُمُ
تَرقُصُ
تَبتَسِمُ

She bequeathed her children
a mother who dreams,
dances,
and smiles.

أُمّاً تبكي
تَعْشَقُ

A mother who weeps
and loves.

أُمّاً لا تَملِكُ مالًا
ولا تَرفو جَوارِبَ

A mother without money
and who doesn't mend socks.

أُمّاً تكتُبُ أشعاراً
بلُغةٍ لا يفهَمُونَها..

A mother who writes poems
in a language they don't understand.

76

خاسِرةٌ
كَمُهرةٍ
امتَطاها فارسٌ
خائبٌ..

She lost out
like a mare
ridden by
a doddering horseman.

77

رَفْرَفَتُ العصافير
خُضرةُ الحديقةِ
التي تُزهرُ
أمامَ عينيها
الهدوءُ
والأيّامُ
التي كانتُ تَمضي
دونَ أن تَرقُصَ
دونَ أن تُغنّي
دونَ أن يَطرُقَ بابها زائرٌ
أو أنْ يرنَّ هاتفُها
ما قتلَها..

The sparrows' singing,
the greenness of the garden
flowering
before her eyes,
the quiet,
and the days
that passed
without her dancing,
without her singing,
without a visitor knocking at her door,
without her phone ever ringing,
is what killed her.

78

لم تكُنْ تُفكّرُ بشيءٍ
أو
هذا ما كانَ يبدو
لم يكُنْ هناكَ مَطَرٌ
ولا عواصفُ شديدةٌ..

She wasn't thinking of anything
or
that's how it seems.
There was no rain pouring down
or severe storms.

لم يكُنْ هناكَ
داعٍ
أو
هذا ما كان يبدو
كي تُمسكَ سِكّيناً
وتقطعَ
شِريانَ ثوبِها..

There was no
reason,
or
that's how it seems,
for her to take a knife
and sever
the arteries of her dress.

80

ثمّةَ عيونٌ
لا ترى الضوءَ
ثمّةَ ذكرياتٌ
لا تُذْكَرُ..

ثمّةَ ابتساماتٌ لا تَمْنَحُ الفَرَحَ
ثمّةَ دموعٌ لا تَغْسِلُ الأَلَمَ
ثمّةَ كلماتٌ تَصفَعُ
ثمّةَ مشاعرُ
ثمّةَ روحٌ
لا عَزاءَ لها..

There are eyes
that see no light,
there are memories
never remembered.

There are smiles that give no joy,
there are tears that wash away no pain.
There are words that slap,
there are feelings,
there is a soul
that cannot be consoled.

82

بخُطى الهِرِّ
الرشيقةِ
بصمتِها
اخطِفْني وهُمْ نِيامٌ..

لا تنسَ أنْ ترسُمَ
ابتسامةً على وجهي
لتهدِّئَ
رَوعَ أطفالي
صباحاً
عندما يُقلقُهُم
غيابي..

With a cat's nimble
silent
steps,
kidnap me as they sleep.

Don't forget to draw
a smile on my face
to calm
the children
in the morning
when my absence
frightens them.

86

تزحَفُ ببطءٍ
لكنْ
بثقةٍ
أَشْعُرُ بها تدنو

أُنصِتُ
إنّها تلهَثُ
كَمَن يحاولُ
تسلُّقَ حائطٍ
أَملَسَ..

She crawls slowly,
but
with confidence.
I feel her coming closer.

I listen.
She is panting
like someone
trying to climb
a slippery wall.

89

مباركٌ بطنُكِ
الملي‌ءُ
بالرغباتِ والخوفِ..
صدرُكِ العارمُ العارمُ الذابلُ..
فمُكِ الذي
يَسيلُ صوتًا
ومياهاً..
أصابعُكِ
التي تكتُبُ
التي تَمسَحُ
التي تبني
التي تَهدِمُ..
مُبَارَكةٌ
شهواتُكِ
وآلامُكِ..
مُباركٌ
عَبَثُكِ..

Blessed is your belly
filled
with wishes and fears,
your robust, crumbled, wilting chest,
your mouth that
drips with sound
and water,
you fingers
that write
that erase
that build
that destroy.
Blessed
your desires
and pains.
Blessed
your futility.

90

أَلَم يكونوا
مشرّدينَ
فآوَيتِ
جِياعاً
فأطعمتِ
خائفينَ
فأسبلتِ على قلوبِهِمْ
الطمأنينةَ
وأنتِ تَعْلَمينَ
أَنَهُمْ
كالعواصِفِ
عابرونْ..

Were they not
destitute
and you housed
the hungry
and fed
the terrified
and spread comfort
about their hearts
knowing
they were
like storms
always passing...

92

يُثقِلُونَ
اكتافَ يوِمها
بكثيرٍ
من قليلٍ
حُبِّهِمْ..

They burden
the shoulders of her day
with a great deal
of their meagre
love.

94

كُلّهُمْ لها
كُلّهُمْ
لها..

They're all hers.
All of them
are hers…

الذينَ
تحبّهم ويحبّونَها
تُحبّهُمْ ولا يُحبّونَها..

Those
she loves and who love her,
she loves and who don't love her.

تأخذُهُم
من أحضانِ أسِرّتِهم
من مشاغِلِهِمْ وهمومِهِمْ
تغسِلُهُمْ
تُعطّرُهُمْ
تُجمّلُهُمْ
يكفي..
أن تُغمِضَ عَيْنَيْها
وتَحلُمْ..

She takes them
from the embraces of their beds,
from their concerns and worries.
She washes them,
perfumes them,
beautifies them.
It suffices her
to close her eyes
and dream.

95

دَعيهِمْ يُقبِلونَ
فوقَ جِمالِهِمْ
مؤمنينَ بالرؤيةِ
يهتِفونَ بِنَجْمَة..

Let them come,
riding their camels,
believing the vision,
guided by the star.

الأبوابُ الموصَدَةُ
ستُفتَحُ
عندما يَسْجدونَ
بتواضُعِ الملوكِ
ليقدِّموا عندَ
سريرِكِ
صلواتِهِمْ..

The shuttered doors
will open.
And they will prostrate
with the humility
of kings
to offer,
by your bedside,
their prayers.

97

كم تُركتَ
لتُصبِحَ فَزِعاً..

How long have you been
abandoned
to be startled so…

كم تألَّمتَ
لتُصبِحَ قاسياً..

How long have you suffered
to have become so cruel…

وكَمْ بينَ هذا
وذاكَ
تُفاجِئُني بكَ
يا حُبّ..

And how long between this
and that
have you surprised me
O love…

98

سامحُو
عَنّي آثارَ الليلِ
بقُطْنٍ
وحليبٍ
وماءٍ وَرْدْ..

سأخلعُ دِفْأَهُ
كثَوْبِ نَوْمي
أرميهِ
على أقربِ كُرسيٍّ
لأستقبلَ
النهارَ
عشيقيَ المُضيءْ..

I will wipe
the traces of the night
off me
with cotton
and milk
and rose water,

I will strip his warmth
like a night-gown
and toss it
on the nearest chair,
to greet
daylight
my luminous lover.

99

كلّما غادَرَني
رَجُلٌ
أَزدادُ جَمالاً..

Whenever a man
leaves me
my beauty increases.

100

أَزدادُ..

Increases...